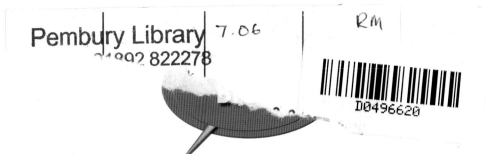

Football

by David Orme

Trailblazers

Football
by David Orme
Educational consultant: Helen Bird

Illustrated by Martin Bolchover and Cyber Media (India) Ltd.

Published by Ransom Publishing Ltd.
Rose Cottage, Howe Hill, Watlington, Oxon. OX49 5HB
www.ransom.co.uk

ISBN   184167 425 7
        978 184167 425 4

First published in 2006

Illustrations copyright © 2006 Martin Bolchover and Ransom Publishing Ltd.

Every effort has been made to locate all copyright holders of material used in this book. If any errors or omissions have occurred, corrections will be made in future editions of this book.

A CIP catalogue record of this book is available from the British Library.

The rights of David Orme to be identified as the author and of Martin Bolchover and Cyber Media (India) Ltd. to be identified as the illustrators of this Work have been asserted by them in accordance with sections 77 and 78 of the Copyright, Design and Patents Act 1988.

Printed in China through Colorcraft Ltd., Hong Kong.

Football

Contents

Football

Get the facts

The world's favourite game!

You can:

  Watch your local team

  Watch the world's best teams on TV

 Play a game of football with your friends

 Collect football stuff

 Play football computer games

or maybe:

 One day you will play for the world's best team!

Football timeline

200 BC	The Romans loved football! They played with a round ball full of hair.	
AD 1300	England went football crazy. A whole village could be used as a pitch! There were no rules and it was very rough.	
1389	The King banned football. He wanted people to practice shooting with bows and arrows.	
1600	Boys in school played football. Every school had its own rules.	

1843	All schools started to use the same rules.
1863	The Football Association (F.A.) was started.
1871	Clubs played the first F.A. Cup matches.
1885	Clubs started to pay their players.
1885	The football league started.
1930	The first World Cup games.

Famous clubs

Los Angeles Galaxy

Founded 1994. MLS (Major League Soccer) Champions 2005.

Mascot: Cozmo, an alien that looks like a frog.

Manchester United

Founded 1878. Greatest players: George Best, Bobby Charlton.

Worst event: The death of 8 players in a plane crash in 1958.

Santos (Sao Paulo)

Founded 1912. Brazilian Champions 2002 and 2004.

Most famous player: Pele. He played for the club for 18 years and scored over 1,000 goals.

Barcelona

Founded 1899. The have won the UEF Cup three times, and the Spanish League 16 times.

Arsenal

Founded 1886 by workers in a factory making guns. Nickname: The Gunners.

League champions 13 times. F.A. Cup Winners 2004/5.

Bayern Munich

Founded 1900. They have won the European Cup 4 times and the German league 17 times.

Most famous player: Franz Beckenbauer.

Ajax Amsterdam

Founded 1900. They have won the European Cup 4 times and the Dutch league an amazing 29 times.

Most famous player: Johann Cryuff.

Juventus (Turin)

Founded 1897. Italy's most successful team. They have won the UEFA Cup three times.

Nickname: 'The Old Lady.'

Famous players

Pele

(born 1940)
Santos FC and Brazil

George Best

(born 1946)
**Manchester United
and Northern Ireland**

Franz Beckenbauer

(born 1945)
**Bayern Munich
and Germany**

Peter Shilton

(born 1949)

**Leicester City
and England**

Bobby Charlton

(born 1937)

**Manchester United
and England**

David Beckham

(born 1975)

**Manchester United,
Real Madrid and
England**

13

The FIFA World Cup™

 When did it start?

In 1930.

 Where was the first World Cup played?

In Uruguay, a country in South America.

 Who won the World Cup in 1930?

The home team of Uruguay. They beat Argentina by 4 goals to 2.

Uruguay won again in 1950.

 Which team has won the cup the most times?

Brazil has won it 5 times.

Italy and Germany have won it 3 times.

What is the cup called?

The first cup was the Jules Rimet Cup. Jules Rimet was the man who started the World Cup. The cup was stolen in 1983. The FIFA World Cup took its place.

© 1974 FIFA TM

The Jules Rimet Cup

The FIFA World Cup Trophy™

When did England win the World Cup?

They won it in 1966 at Wembley stadium in London. They beat West Germany by 4 goals to 2.

Football quiz

Can you answer these questions?

Reading this book will help you with some of the answers.

1 **Which team is known as the Gunners?**
- Manchester United
- Arsenal
- Glasgow Rangers

2 **When did Manchester United start playing?**
- 1878
- 1965
- 1888

3 **Can you name a famous team from Spain?**
- Real Madrid
- Bayern Munich
- Inter Milan

4 **When did the World Cup start?**
- 1871
- 1885
- 1930

5 **What happened to the World Cup in 1983?**

What country was the first World Cup played in?

6
- England
- Spain
- Uruguay

Why did the King stop people playing football in 1389?

7
- He hated football
- Too many people were getting hurt
- He wanted them to practice with bows and arrows

What song do Liverpool supporters sing? Is it

8
- Rock Around the Clock
- You'll Never Walk Alone
- What a Useless Referee

Which of these players was a famous England goalkeeper?

9
- Peter Shilton
- George Best
- Bobby Charlton

Which of these teams *hasn't* David Beckham played for?

10
- Real Madrid
- Arsenal
- Manchester United

The answers are on the next page.   17

Football quiz - answers:

1 Arsenal

2 1878

3 Real Madrid

4 1930

5 Someone stole it

6 Uruguay

7 He wanted them to practice with bows and arrows

8 You'll Never Walk Alone

9 Peter Shilton

10 Arsenal

Rob
of the
Rovers

Chapter 1:
A bad season

It was a bad season for Rovers. Unless they won the final match they would go down to Division Two.

Bill Tonks, the manager, got some bad news just before the match. Mick Speedy, their best striker, was in jail! There had been a fight in a night club and Mick had started it. Without him, they had no chance!

Then Bill remembered the professor.

The professor was a football fan. Bill Tonks thought he was a total nutter. He had shown Bill a football playing robot called Rob 1. It was a brilliant player, but it looked like a heap of junk.

"If my robot played for Rovers, you would be top of the league!" said the professor.

"If that thing played for us, we would be chucked out of the league!" said Bill.

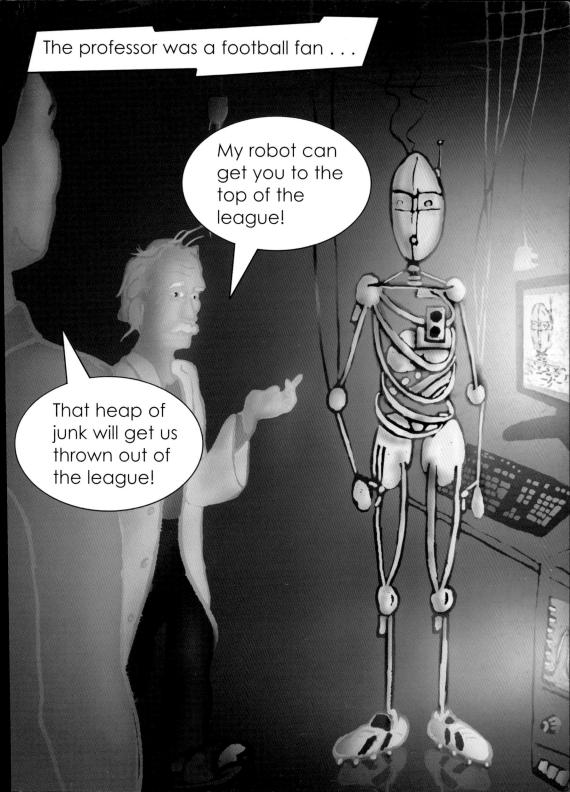

Chapter 2:
Rob gets a chance

The professor told Bill that Rob 1 was only a trial. The next one would look like a real player.

Bill was desperate. The rules didn't allow robots to play, but if it looked really human, no one would find out. He picked up the phone and called the professor.

"I'm going to give the robot a chance," he said.

The professor brought Rob 2 to a training session. The other players didn't know he was a robot.

"This is Rob Steel," said Bill. "He's a new signing."

Rob didn't say much but he had all the skills. "The more he plays, the better he gets," said the professor.

Bill wished all his players were robots. Robots don't go to night clubs.

Chapter 3:
The final match

It was the final match. Rovers were playing City. They had to beat them to stay up.

Bill was nervous. Rob hadn't played in a match before. But he began well. He scored three times in the first half. City didn't know what had hit them.

"He'll be even better in the second half," said the professor. "He keeps on learning."

The final match of the season. Could Rovers stay up?

In the second half the Rovers crowd were cheering like mad for Rob. The professor was right. The more he played, the better he got.

He ran faster and tackled harder. He seemed to be everywhere. He could pick up the ball from anywhere on the field, and no-one could keep up with him. The crowd loved it.

But the professor was worried.

The fans thought Rob was great . . .
Goal!
. . . but the professor wasn't happy.

Chapter 4:
Better all the time

"I programmed him to learn, and get better," he whispered to Bill. "But I forgot to program him to stop getting better!"

Things began to go wrong for Rovers. Rob was too good. No human could run as fast as he did, or kick the ball as hard. The score was 15 - nil to Rovers.

"Slow him down!" hissed Bill.

But the professor couldn't.

Rob was too good to be human . . .
Slow him down!
I forgot to program him to *stop* getting better!
The score was 15 - nil to Rovers!

Rob was now running so fast he was just a blur. The City goalie had run off – it was too dangerous in goal. The ref. kept blowing his whistle but Rob was too fast to hear it.

At last he slowed down and stopped.

The ref waved a red card.

"Off!" he yelled.

"Can't. Flat battery." Rob croaked, just before he fell over with a crash.